Margaret W. J. W. Mitchell
December 16, 1985

The ZEN HAIKU
and other ZEN POEMS
of J. W. HACKETT

The ZEN HAIKU
and other ZEN
POEMS
of J. W. HACKETT

JAPAN PUBLICATIONS, INC.

This book is a completely revised and enlarged edition of *The Way of
Haiku: An Anthology of Haiku Poems* including new Zen poems.

Published by JAPAN PUBLICATIONS, INC.

Distributors:
UNITED STATES: *Kodansha International/USA, Ltd., through Harper & Row,
Publishers, Inc., 10 East 53rd Street, New York, N.Y. 10022.* SOUTH AMERICA:
Harper & Row, Publishers, Inc., International Department. CANADA: *Fitzhenry
& Whiteside Ltd., 150 Lesmill Road, Don Mills, Ontario M3B 2T6.* MEXICO
AND CENTRAL AMERICA: *HARLA S. A. de C. V., Apartado 30–546, Mexico
4, D. F.* BRITISH ISLES: *International Book Distributors Ltd., 66 Wood Lane
End, Hemel Hempstead, Herts HP2 4RG.* EUROPEAN CONTINENT: *Boxerbooks,
Inc., Limmatstrasse 111, 8031 Zurich.* AUSTRALIA AND NEW ZEALAND: *Book
Wise (Australia) Pty. Ltd., 101 Argus Street, Cheltenham Vic. 3192.* THE FAR
EAST AND JAPAN: *Japan Publications Trading Co., 1–2–1, Sarugaku-cho,
Chiyoda-ku, Tokyo 101.*

First Printing: August 1983

ISBN 0–87040–533–0

Printed in Japan

PREFACE

Bashō (1643–94), the most famous Japanese haiku poet, was studying Zen under the guidance of Master Bucchō. One day, it is said, the master asked Bashō, "What is the Buddha Dharma of today?" Bashō replied, "After the rain, the green moss gets wet." The master further asked, in order to test the depth of Bashō's insight, "How about before the rain, before the moss gets wet?" Bashō replied, "A frog jumps in the water, the sound of the water!" This is the beautiful Zen dialogue through which Bashō expressed his understanding of Zen. Later, after much struggle, Bashō added, "The old pond, ah!" Thus it became seventeen syllables: a haiku.

When the original,

> *Furu ike ya!*
> *Kawazu tobikomu*
> *Mizu no oto.*

—is translated into English:

> The old pond, ah!
> A frog jumps in:
> The water's sound!

—someone in the South, say Louisiana, who has never been to Japan, and who knows only the kind of frog that is bigger than the palm of his hand, and which makes a *terrific* sound when it jumps into the water, will naturally get a corresponding image. Japanese people read it with the experience of frogs that are almost tiny, and accordingly make a small, sharp sound. Thus, as far as the image is concerned, the Louisiana image and the Japanese image are quite different. But we cannot say that people from Louisiana do not understand haiku or that they do not understand Zen.

When Bashō replied to Master Bucchō's question, he did not specify that the frog was tiny or that the sound was sharp. Let us ask Bucchō to repeat his question to Bashō: "How about before the rain, before the moss gets wet?" Even if Bashō said exactly the same thing, but with the image that the frog is bigger than the palm of his hand, he is still expressing his Zen.

Although haiku is the shortest poetic form, shorter than any traditional Western form, it can also be written in English, and French too, and the resulting condensed expression is no other than the expression of Zen. The essence of haiku is the essence of Zen, which freely passes across cultural and linguistic boundaries.

James W. Hackett, known as "America's Bodhidharma," is—like Bodhidharma—a pioneer, for he wrote these haiku in English with the faith that English-language haiku will be, and is indeed becoming, as R. H. Blyth said of Japanese haiku, "The expression of a temporary enlightenment . . . a way in which the cold winter rain, the swallows of evening, even the very day in its hotness and the length of the night become truly alive, share in our humanity, speak their own silent and expressive language."

EIDO TAI SHIMANO
Dai Bosatsu Zendo
November 5, 1982

FOREWORD AND COMMENTS
BY R. H. BLYTH

These remarkably good haiku by Mr. Hackett cannot be made to seem better than they are by any praise of mine, but I would like to emphasize the fact that, like the best haiku of the Japanese poets, they are not so much literature, or even poetry in the ordinary sense of the word, as direct communications of poetical experiences; not "the best words," but the right words; more like the music of Bach than the music of Schubert.

To attain this ability, to express the immediate sensation, to pour all of one's self into the thing, and let the thing penetrate every part of one's self, needs much travail of mind and body. It requires also the renunciation of all ambition to be "recognised," though some few persons must share the experiences to as to assure, if possible, their universal validity. In Mr. Hackett's case, I am one of those persons, who can never be many, but who, as Emerson tells us, are the really important people in the world —though I says it as shouldn't.

I think these verses as good as, and sometimes better than those of the higher ranks of haiku poets of the past. All of the haiku appeal to me strongly, for different reasons. I found a feeling of regret creeping over me as I read through the verses . . . and when I thought what it arose from, I realised that it was that Bashō should not have you for his pupil (and he as your pupil) instead of the rather mediocre disciples he actually had.

You yourself are a very lucky man, I mean lucky like Christ was, or Bashō was, to be born a poet just at the right time. (I myself am the luckiest person I know, you shall be the next.)

AUTHOR'S INTRODUCTION

The haiku poems in this book are original creations in English and are not translations. Neither are they mere imitations of Japanese haiku. Each poem reflects my own experience with nature, in my garden and in the wilds of America. I have written in the conviction that the best haiku are created from direct and immediate experience with nature, and that this intuitive experience can be expressed in any language. In essence I regard haiku as fundamentally existential and experiential, rather than literary. There are, of course, important structural and artistic considerations involved in the expression of the haiku experience, and these I discuss in my suggestions at the end of this book. It was, however, the spiritual qualities of haiku which prompted me to adapt it to English.

It is haiku's sense of the real which above all else justifies its universal adaptation. Of all poetry, haiku is the one which best holds a mirror up to nature. Characteristic of true haiku is a spirit of *suchness*, wherein nature is reflected just as it is. Since lifefulness, not beauty, is to me the real quality of haiku, the reader should bear in mind that my poems are not intended to captivate with art. They seek rather to reveal, by reflection, the wonders of natural creation. I am a life worshipper, not an apostle of poetry or art; it is to lifefulness that my poems aspire. I have long believed that haiku's real treasure is its touchstone of the present . . . the very pulse of life itself.

Years of living and writing haiku experiences have convinced me that haiku should not be regarded as just a literary art. Haiku is more than a form of poetry. I discovered it can be a way of living awareness—a way of Zen which leads to wonder and joy, and through the discovery of our essential identity, to compassion for all forms of life.

I leave it to the reader to decide whether the way of haiku is relevant to him. Certainly there are many ways, and like the others, haiku has meaning for the individual who is ready for what it offers and demands.

Man has not expunged greater nature; individuals have only isolated themselves from it. The modern city is a concrete monument to man's conceit and insensitivity. Fortunately, life is change. Science has begun to recognize that a microcosmic, man-centered view of the world is not only shortsighted, but dangerous. There is reason to hope that communities of the future will begin to reflect our aesthetic and spiritual need for the rest of nature.

Haiku as a way, however, involves more than place of being, or even a macrocosmic view of life. To me it is ultimately a Zen state of mind—a way of living each moment as if it were our last. It is a way which seeks to improve the quality of our life experience. In the final analysis I believe that it is far more important to live with haiku awareness than to write haiku poems. When the reader closes my book with greater appreciation and awareness of *this moment of life,* then its purpose will have been fulfilled.

J. W. H.

ACKNOWLEDGMENTS

I am deeply grateful: to my old Buddhist friend and poet John Farr, but for whom I might never have begun to create; to my mentor and friend R. H. Blyth, from whose inspired and monumental volumes on Japanese haiku and Zen I learned so much . . . whatever I have written simply would not be, but for his encouragement through those years when there was none; to D. T. Suzuki, Sohaku Ogata, and Nyogen Senzaki whose great dedication to Zen helped me to see the Way; to my friend Sōen Nakagawa, in whose company many rare pleasures were shared; to my dear wife Pat, for the time to find, and for all her invaluable help, suggestions, and typing assistance; to Anne Lee Smith whose loyalty, kindness, and suggestions have greatly helped; to Harold G. Henderson and other loyal supporters who have respected what I have tried to do; to those kindred spirits Thoreau, Bashō, and the Chinese poets (especially Wang Wêi, Tu Fu and Po Chü-i), all of whom have deeply enriched my loneliness; and certainly to my pets Zen, Haiku, Sakè, Kabuki, Krishna, Karma, Blyth Spirit, Bodhidharma, Han Shan, Pu Tai, Ladybug, and Chō Chō, in whose loving and enlightened company I have found such inspiration and pleasure; finally, to the Ancient One above all, and in the case of you, nothing needs to be said—though I says it as I should.

J. W. H.
November 1982

CONTENTS

TO THIS ETERNAL NOW

Fall ranges beyond . . .
   and here for our mountain breath,
      the ease of heather.

Rooted in boulder:
   once borne, now gnarled into form
      by the summit wind.

With every gust of sun,
   a halo of golden down
      surrounds the hawk.

Searching on the wind,
   the hawk's cry . . .
      is the shape of its beak.

3

The trail overgrown,
  I'll take the way of this creek
    now silenced into sand.

A leaf in mid-air,
  the way it spins to a stand . . .
    then begins again.

In a dry creek bed:
  a sparrow bathing in sand
    amid tracks of thirst.

An elusive deer
  wandering through autumn leaves:
    the taste of tea.

Many strains of sparrow
there are, yet the same fall theme
graces them all.

Abandoned cabin
all askew, boasting a roof
of deep autumn leaves.

The web rising free
from the rim of this lantern,
dances with my breath!

In this howling night
of wind, the full moon alone
seems to be unmoved.

Leaving the ridge
    to racing hikers, streaked with sweat,—
    the way of the stream.

Sun plays on the stream,
    and reflects on every tree
    its shimmering dance!

Tumbling upstream
    against the racing current—
    a downy, white seed.

Wind gives way to calm,
    and the stream smoothes, revealing
    its treasure of leaves . . .

This sunny shallow
   so warm and softened by silt,
      clouds . . . with a touch.

Bathing off the trail,
   by a fall full of rainbows . . .
      in harmony unknown.

Come, lie in this stream . . .
   all the sun of summer gone
      is within its flow.

This leaf too, with all
   its colors eaten into lace,
      floats on the stream.

The fall roars from cloud
   down the canyon wall . . . then ends
   in a maze of rainbows!

Heron's heavy flight
   alights into a standing grace
   before the falls . . .

Deep within the stream
   the huge fish lie motionless,
   facing the current.

Among these mountains,
   I've lost my longing to live
   in an ancient time.

The tall smoke rising
   from the cabin far below,
     now centers a hawk . . .

But for a loud spire,
   the valley village has become
     a silent cloud.

A quiet crossroads . . .
   on the door of an empty store:
     "Opportunity Shop."

Riding snout out
   with eyes closed by the wind
     in a world of smells!

This tideless silence . . .
    yet unheard, but for the screech
      of a searching gull.

In this tide pool,
    crawling out of a crushed crab—
      several little ones.

On nearing the surf,
    every footprint becomes
      that of the sea.

The swooping eagle
    waits till his talons clutch the fish
      to break his great wings!

The fleeing sandpipers
  turn about suddenly
    and chase back the sea!

Touched by the tide
  huddled crabs scatter, and fight . . .
    the hunger of the sea.

Over this smooth beach
  between each wash of the moon,—
    our vanishing prints.

The eagle lofts away
  lifting his prey with wings
    that stir the sea!

Look, last night's wind
   has set the whole garden ablaze
      with bougainvillea!

They come separately,
   and then leave the garden as one
      giant butterfly.

Two flies, so small
   it's a wonder they ever met,
      are mating on this rose.

The pursued beetle
   just led the other into
      an empty snail shell!

Just an old leaf, yet
  try to follow its structure—
  or count its colors!

Butterfly's splendor
  folds into a tall silence
  upon the flower.

Blooming, with an edge
  already withering . . . this life,
  this constant death.

Snail may creep his way,
  but see how he binds with silver
  each moment he leaves.

Sunrise . . . unseen till now,
the strands of web that unite
each flower and bough.

Sly black butterfly—
your stunts always seem to end
on a marigold.

What wealth can compare
to this tea stillness, these walnuts,
and slices of orange!

Sometimes the oddest thing,
like this orange pip,
begs not to be thrown away.

Old chestnut breaks the walk,
   but scatters leaves for the child
     stepping safe from cracks.

Puppy's silent paws
   allow him to romp right up to
     butterflies on the walk!

Already becoming
   a family of beetle:
     dawn's unseen snail.

That old empty house,
   now overgrown with years,
     is the only real one here.

A gusty morning . . .
    wading wantonly through leaves,
        the sound of autumn.

My fanciful kitten—
    scrambling after a leaf
        she's already caught.

Rare waxwing, you need
    but perch for a moment
        to make the world your friend!

In the crystal air
    after every gust of wind—
        an autumn carnival!

A deep autumn path,
     with not a soul to be seen . . .
         ancient loneliness.

Gentle falling leaf,
     your meander through the air
         holds everything.

Autumn evening . . .
     the weight and shape of this moment
         is a distant bell.

Without beginning
     or end, the silvery trail
         that designs this walk.

The sprig to her taste,
  the cat sits in the midst of chaos—
    cleaning herself.

Sweeping into a pan:
  the narrow line of dust
    that defies its edge.

This speck on the page
  that blowing doesn't remove,
    has a mind of its own!

Romping new puppy
  sits down every so often
    and whimpers awhile.

All of a sudden
autumn clings to the window . . .
and then disappears.

Look at this fly that
long since met eternity—
his kneeling remains.

Beneath white roses
on a polished table . . .
petals lie in dust.

With death's arrival,
this present moment alone
becomes known as real.

A bitter morning:
    sparrows sitting together
        without any necks.

Wintry wind now sweeps
    the trees, touching the same leaves
        never . . . and again.

Beside a new grave . . .
    burdened with the crushing weight
        of ungiven love.

Always calming, now
    an ease even to grief:
        my koi and goldfish friends.

A distant dog
   is adding another shade of gray
     to the morning.

After a night of wind,
   winter stands everywhere . . .
     over autumn ground.

Tightening the sky
   already taut with gray:
     a slow-wheeling hawk.

The wounded deer drinks,
   and its reflection becomes
     a crimson cloud . . . .

Winter desolation . . .
  the breast of the waiting hawk
  tufts up with each wind.

Gently falling snow
  lays over the still deer
  a mantle of oneness.

The swooping silence
  of the hawk, breaks with a shriek
  —just above its prey.

A snow-darkened stream:
  yellow moon upon a bough
  melting . . . into moon.

Rocks stacked high with snow
    narrow this wild stream into
        smooth ribbons of flow . . .

Chopping kindling from
    a knotty block . . . in each stick,
        a part of its shape.

The icicle grows,
    only to blunt itself
        on the frozen ground.

Deep winter, and yet
    the chickadee still chirps and sings
        his cheerfulness!

In every barren tree
    hang wonders of frosty web
      for the Christmas sun!

Viewing new snow . . .
    the shape of my loneliness,
      every winter breath.

In this silent snow,
    each crunching step echoes dryly
      into my teeth.

Another sermon—
    wafting through words without end,
      the smell of coffee.

Now, with each avalanche
of snow from the branches—
an excited bird!

Melting sun . . . one by one
boughs of the cedar spring back
into its contour.

A brown, tinseled tree
standing beside garbage cans
in a melting world.

Spring! the warbler sings,
with an exuberance that
sometimes spreads his wings.

I

An old country inn . . .
a tearoom beamed with timbers
and spring morning sun.

II

Leaded windows opened
to fragrant blossoms, and a
warbler lost in song . . .

III

Walnut woods, mellow
with years, graced by the lustre
of unadorned silver!

IV

Sketches of rustic themes . . .
the private song of the girl
preparing our tea.

Broken last winter,
    this branch dangling by a strand
        is full of blossom!

The tender green of these
    new leaves among the blossoms
        delights the fingers . . .

Sprightly chickadee
    so full of cheer, never comes
        except as a pair.

This gentle spring breeze
    now is wafting a scent
        from another world!

Iris blues flecked with
   silver like the dawn give way to
      a burst of grandeur.

Kinglet's busyness—
   unlike chickadee's, has an edge
      from being alone.

Ladybug, you turn
   every dew you pass into
      an amber jewel!

Dew gathered by dawn:
   an elixir—favored
      by the ladybug.

Fly, fledgling robin . . .
 your thumping breast alone
  strands you from the sky.

Each blossom of plum
 speeds the bumblebee's hum
  into a loud buzz!

The spider dangles,
 waiting for wind to swing him
  to another limb.

Wisteria, so rich alone,
 now with yellow warbler—
  a Chinese scroll, and poem.

The pauses within
　　robin's song to the dawn
　　　　are long draughts of dew.

Such a humble bloom
　　on the ivy, and yet see
　　　　how it draws the bees!

At the end of a thread
　　dancing around in mid-air:
　　　　a tiny larva.

This blessed present,
　　wherever I look I see
　　　　nothing—but Buddha.

The spring that lost
   its identity in the rain,
      is a song again.

Blossoms that held bees
   now leave with the gentle breeze
      from butterfly wings.

In this cloudless sky,
   drifting white petals alone
      give the wind a way.

Ending, worlds after
   being dislodged by the bee:
      the petal shower.

Suburban morning . . .
a new suit of clothes, planning
a trip into town.

To unhook his claw,
the old cat just tugs and tugs
until it is free.

The finicky cat
bites his new food, then tastes it
looking far away.

The door held for her,
the cat stops on the threshold
and sniffs the jamb . . .

God must have been
    feeling very frivolous
        when He created the cat.

Supporting himself,
    in an original comedy . . .
        the lone parakeet.

My bird just listens
    to most music, but whistles
        and sings with Mozart!

In an open drawer,
    smoothing out a rough day:
        a sleeping kitten.

An apple core, just
short of the sea's surging wash:
caravanning ants.

Crow pecks into the sand,
swallows what he finds, then
shudders all over!

"Mike what tore your pants?
"Susan don't eat sand!"—all this
in a single breath!

The gull drops his clam,
and flies off with my apple core . . .
a family feast?

Sea horse no sooner
  sucks in a fish, than he spits out
    its whole skeleton!

Vigorously shaking
  the paw of the kitten—
    an adventurous ant.

The bane of sea gulls
  seeking clams they've dropped on rocks:
    their own fresh poop.

The ants on this cloth
  are even carrying off
    their own casualties.

Summer verandah . . .
   listening to fluttering birds:
     the tail of the cat.

To lift her fledgling
   safety-high . . . took two big worms,
     and a dragonfly!

Now centered upon
   the flavor of an old bone,
     the mind of my dog.

Despite everything
   I honor you common fly—
     master of the air!

Sparrow bathes in warmth,
   but wades out to the cool fount
    to sate his thirst.

Little ladybug
   hides under her lovely shell
    a pair of long wings.

Each bud of iris,
   although tightly sheathed in green,
    hints the hue within.

Even while squatting
   the puppy diverts herself
    by smelling flowers.

Summer heat . . . the cat
   sits down in the breeze behind
     the happy puppy.

Krishna takes my lap,
   and his purring now becomes
     my meditation.

Upon hearing me
   intone the sacred "OM" . . .
     how startled my cat!

Long since a playmate,
   but always tagging along:
     the old cat's shadow.

Trapped within the house,
  this fly chose to die clinging
    to my vased weed.

Bumblebee bumping
  against the window . . . something
    you want me to see?

This spider so still
  on the window sill, has been
    made a part of it.

The lone parakeet
  nudges his hanging mirror,
    then watches it move . . .

Dry pasture, ribboned
   by the flowers and butterflies
     of a hidden spring . . .

Cricket chews the grass
   till it starts to give way, then
     wings to another.

The indifference
   within the cow's chewing stare—
     stops our hilarity.

A road dancing with heat,
   through acre after acre
     of Mexican hats.

Rare wine for the eye:
the bougainvillea, flowering
this ancient mission.

Wherever I look
within this blue summer wind,
I can find a seed.

The more sparrow climbs
toward the top of that reed—
the lower he gets.

The small girl picking
wild flowers, suddenly flies
into a wild dance!

The dreaded thistle,
    for all of its many spines,
        is a host to bugs.

A roaring waterfall:
    eucalyptus trees tossing
        the summer wind.

Now—even filled with pain
    from this thorn in my finger—
        is so good to feel!

An abandoned board—
    shaping, sunning, becoming
        a bug Shangrila.

The grasshopper springs,
    and catches the summer wind
        with his outstretched wings.

Random flies meet,
    cling together, and fall buzzing
        into the rank grass.

Snail falls; then slowly
    rights himself shell and all
        by grasping a straw.

This garter snake
    goes in and out of the grass
        all at the same time!

One thistle, so purple
it echoes across the creek
unseen shades of green . . .

Wherever this limb
lies within the stream, its form
becomes flowing moss . . .

One minnow in this shallow
has blown for himself a
big bubble—lookout.

Did you periwinkles,
creeping on some old creek bed,
inspire "Birnam Wood?"

Dents from my nail
  left deep around this bite, alone
  relieve its madness!

Losing in its bout
  with the pesky fly: the ear
  of the sleeping fawn.

Peeing seclusion . . .
  coated with dust and pine needles,
  a melon rind pleads.

Burning stones border
  warm shallows . . . a fish tugs at
  the old angler's dream.

Mice run the old mill,
  deer browse within its walls . . .
    ripe berries roll the shoot.

All of the large rocks
  rushing this stream, have wet lines
    above the surface.

Crossing the rapids . . .
  on the next rock some scat lies
    challenging the sole.

Old grandad one-claw
  quiets the fighting crayfish
    with just his presence!

Within this hollow seed,
and all the time around it:
the shape of emptiness.

Now at journey's end,
circling the shallow stream . . .
years of open sea.

Wind sounds the trees . . .
while here, gnats play in the calm
of wooded sunlight.

Gradually moving
the whole forest to silence,
an enchanted bird.

The sparrow bathes—
  showering into the sunlight
    thousands of jewels!

Need friends ever speak?
  There's tea to taste, and windsong
    from the garden trees.

A long line of web
  unseen, but for shifting stretches
    that return the sun.

The stillness of the seed
  soon turns the spider back
    into seclusion.

Gnats come as a cloud,
   and then spread out over
      the coolness of the pool.

The playful kitten—
   how calmly he chews the fly's
      buzzing misery.

A tiny spider
   has begun to confiscate
      this cup's emptiness.

Summer dusk . . . the birds
   gather in one tree and share
      the day's excitement!

Rain drums on the pane
 and runs down, wavering the world
  into a dream.

Reading this sutra,
 I suddenly began to laugh . . .
  without knowing why.

The kitten crouches,
 and then leaps at the genie
  rising from the tea.

Just in from the rain,
 my wet shaggy dog smells
  like fifty dry ones!

No longer a kitten,
    the cat now pounces on my hand
    clawlessly . . .

Still on this bath tub:
    the little bug that I had
    promised a flower.

From one floating hair:
    a chain of shadows, all bound
    by links of bright light.

Flashing neon night
    blurred through a steamy window:
    a concert of colors!

Through the gossamer wings
of this still dragonfly . . .
the blooming cosmos.

The spider spins round
and round his ancient design,
bound for the center.

Deep in the rank grass:
a rusty toy truck, with a
cargo of cocoons.

Time after time
caterpillar climbs this broken stem
—then probes beyond.

The caterpillar
    walks his rear legs first, to raise
        the slack that moves him.

That long drop of dew
    must have been held by my
        attention alone!

The sound of this spring
    washing over mossy rocks,
        holds a butterfly.

Here where the spring waits,
    a treasure of stones appears
        deep within the moon.

Chattering nonsense
  from my bird Vouchee, now holds
  all I care to know.

The weird, funny world
  mirrored on my puppy's eye,
  eggs the onlooker.

The poet possessed—
  stands with hands on his hips,
  peeing impatiently.

Asked to explain Zen—
  my puppy with the same name
  looks, and thumps his tail.

Think this mite is small?
    Look close . . . what you really see
        is his dawn shadow!

When I mouth new sounds
    for fun, my dogs run to see
        if I'm in trouble!

The puppy's wonder
    tilts his head, first to one side
        and then the other.

On wiping up wet
    puppy shit: the gagging smell . . .
        right now, this is it.

A gull flying low
above a deserted beach,
racing its shadow.

An abandoned book . . .
skimming through its pages,
breezes from the sea.

Cast upon the sand
behind an ebbing wave . . .
hovering shadow.

The derelict scow
answers the mocking frogs with
its timbers of bloom!

Although buried,
   with only oarlocks above the sand,
   its form remains.

These barnacled rocks
   just uncovered by the tide . . .
   how busy they sound!

One fly just flew up
   from the busy dung, to sit
   and wash on my page.

Crow leaves the sea gulls
   clamoring after the tide
   and goes surfboarding!

Slighted by daylight,
but ruling the summer dusk—
the white butterfly.

The expanse of clouds
now lit by this rising moon:
sand rippled by waves.

Night shades disappear,
and within each dew begins
a play of hues . . .

Dawn: in the shadow
cast by every drop of dew,
a burning jewel!

My pillow, sweet grass . . .
   my view, a cloud ever changing,
      ever the same.

Each sunlit bloom
   becomes even more rare when seen
      against its fate.

The little green bug
   crawling out of this flower
      sports new white shoes.

This woolly larva
   has hung himself out to dry
      between two wet leaves!

The small child's errand,
   vies with the wonders he finds
   all along the way.

Beetle commandeers
   some old snail armour, then runs
   across the sidewalk.

Snail, your confusion
   has covered the pavement with
   an exquisite design!

The honeysuckle—
   hummingbird backs out, pauses,
   then goes in again.

My mouser cat, though
   merciless with flies, just sits
     and blinks at the bee.

Ever suspended
   above the ground that he strolls,
     the daddy-longlegs.

Blocked, the line of ants
   just broadens until it can
     go around, and on . . .

Robin pecked into
   that ripe cherry, and now
     he can't get rid of it!

Sweltering city . . .
    echoing through an alley,
        the slaps of hopscotch.

A child's loud laughter;
    doing a dance on the line—
        some full, empty pants.

One kid in the dump
    just yelled to his playmates: "Look,
        a flying saucer!"

Always there when needed:
    the invisible playmate
        of the crippled child.

Breaking gray pavement
  in a hard world, full of words:
    a flowering weed.

Behind the market
  searching through cans of garbage:
    a face of sores.

Writ in weird letters
  across a brick building,—
    the signature of a quake.

Now stores, the orchard
  with summer grasses, boy-high . . .
    where I played and dreamed.

For a real measure
of the day's heat, see the length
of the sleeping cat.

Before he lies down
on the floor, the dog paws away
centuries of leaves.

The sleeping dog's wind
first awakens him . . . and then
drives him from the room.

When finally caught,
the kitten's tail is given
a real good licking.

The kitten's great yawn
　goes all around the room . . .
　　and back again.

A black jewel,
　set in down of the softest blue :
　　my parakeet's eye.

Butterfly flutters
　right through the house, waking up
　　the cat on his way !

Rewarded with food,
　the pup now goes out and squats
　　in ten minute shifts.

Heavy summer rain,—
   but to the fledgling just the time
    to practise his song.

Waves of winded rain
   sweep over the flooded street,
    designing its flow.

Rain comes to an end,
   and the half-finished house
    shouts and swears again.

Rain's run-off design:
   cascades of clear pavement gray
    led by yellow swells!

Sun just after rain:
a song from every bird . . .
the fresh smell of greens.

Ants bearing white loads
are flooding the dry portions
of this puddled walk.

Yesterday's creaking wind . . .
now is a butterfly
poised on a flower.

Fingers love to feel
themselves, after touching
the spire of the lily.

Sauntering home
    with everything in hand:
    a bare first grader.

The "quack quack quack" of
    the neighborhood luny—sounds
    more duck than his duck!

The long bout between
    the walnut and the jay, ends
    in a split decision.

Amid tall grasses,
    one blade waves frantically,—
    a lumbering snail.

Somehow, some spider
  lowered himself to this flower
    from out of the sky!

All the butterflies
  pass the flowers by, to draw
    from that homely weed.

On hitting a stone
  thrown in the air—the triumph;
    the jar from the bat!

When tired of hearing
  the crow's caw, caw, caw—
    just call it back to him!

Unheard and unseen
   while I wandered memory:
   the rush of this stream.

Mountain loneliness . . .
   in every ripe blackberry:
   a smack of tartness.

My reflection now
   swept by wind, I see nothing
   but a constant flow . . .

A leaf on the stream
   sinks slowly through the current
   to the deepest pool.

A miracle of grace:
　　the great blue heron
　　　unfolding into flight.

As the fall sounds near,
　　the turbulent stream smoothes out
　　　and reflects the sky . . .

The mountain stream spills
　　into the wind . . . then below,
　　　finds itself again.

Stormy mountain night . . .
　　following a way revealed
　　　by moments of day.

Waking . . . amid grasses
and wild flowers bright with dew:
cold mountain sunrise.

Sprinkling relief
over a rock by the trail . . .
its hidden colors!

Ceasing his sweet song,
the woodpecker takes a poop,
and then sings again.

A black bear fishes
the stream, while her restless cubs
harass the beaver.

A cloud of bugs
　　busy going nowhere
　　　in a ray of sun.

Bright red whiskers,
　　and a polka dot waistcoat:
　　　the flicker's disguise!

Too subtle to notice
　　anywhere else: the yellow
　　　of the blackbird's eye.

Busy flycatcher
　　always returns to that
　　　old gray limb he matches.

Twilight mountains,
  drifting on a quiet lake . . .
  fish kissing the moon.

In the campfire light:
  the hungry eyes of the child
  vie with drowsiness.

Mountains take the moon,
  and embers cool . . . revealing
  a sky deep with stars.

A single cricket
  is warming the quiet
  of this lonely night.

Beyond valleys dark,
   the dawn now breaks on a flight
     that wings to the sea . . .

Heron takes to flight,
   waking mountain reflections
     with a dangling leg.

Cranes swath through reeds
   in chase . . . while the lake forest
     roars of mating bears.

(in a mountain pond)

From the floundering bug,
   spread rings of desperation . . .
     the greatest—the last.

In a glen too green
    for butterflies . . . the color
    of sweet robin's song!

An abandoned orchard . . .
    limbs laden to tall grasses
    capture emptiness.

The grasshopper's game:
    to light on the tip of a grass,
    then ride out the sway!

Hawk stops with a squawk!
    then drops with eager talons
    —into his shadow.

On the highway:
 a moment of agony, flattened
  and cleansed by time.

Of all the blackbirds,
 this one remaining behind—
  isn't completely.

An old spider web
 low above the forest floor,
  sagging full of seeds.

Giant redwood trees
 vying for the sun and sky,
  —the shade they cast below.

Across this window
of glare, the eave now shadows
a cool mountain view.

Eucalyptus trees
with all their greens whispering . . .
the scent of summer.

Over trampled weeds
and grasses—a tall thistle
seeding summer breeze.

Deer track the stream bed
with thirst, and cries of searching cranes
echo the gorge . . .

Poppies pine for sun . . .
    to weeds, even a gray day
        deserves a flower.

Used as a sofa
    by the zany blackbird—
        the back of the sheep.

A derelict car
    amid grazing nonchalance . . .
        the way of haiku.

Within every seed
    drifting from the thistle:
        a promise of growth.

(in a vacant lot)

A garbage can lid
   left by some fanciful child,
      drumming drops of rain.

A heavy night fog
   has so silenced the city,·
      each light seems a friend.

A yellow streetlight
   haloing . . . into a gray
      drifting nothingness.

Lights give depth to this fog . . .
   some are bright, and others dim,
      all of them lonely.

A morning mass tolls
    stirring the fog . . . my searching eyes
        rest upon nothing.

Free at last, the fly
    flew out the window—and then
        right back in again.

Emerging from fog . . .
    a world of sun and colors,
        heralded by birds!

Robin's raspy song
    smoothes into sweetness after
        every drink of dew.

Moments of dew
drop from the flower, then slow
to one . . . prolonged.

Through a sunlit leaf:
the dark shadows of two bugs
merge and become one.

You crafty spider,
running a web that clings
—to everything else.

The dragonfly's grip
allows him to rest in wind
in spite of his wings!

Weary of wonder,
  I concentrate my view as through
  a dragonfly's wing.

Still a friend to my hand,
  this butterfly, though the wind
  demands his wings.

For the real grandeur
  of the iris, bend so near
  you can see but one.

Pampas grass offers
  such strokeable plumes, to hands
  that will dare its leaves.

Gray memories silenced
    by a gull: the roar of surf . . .
    this cloudless blue!

Gulls heavy with sun
    swoop down over breaking waves
    and wing through the spray.

Walking toward surf . . .
    the pilings of an old pier
    now stump the sand.

Gusts of ocean wind
    wander this deserted beach,
    drifting all . . . to one.

The sovereign eagle,
    searching from cloud with an eye
        that fathoms the sea!

Seaweed in the tide
    takes the shape of each swell
        until stilled by sand.

The evening tide
    lapping around these pilings,
        rests with barnacles.

Moving slowly through
    an old, abandoned beach house . . .
        shadows of the moon.

A white tapping cane,
   revealing a world of colors
      to passersby.

Buildings hide the sky
   and pavement the earth, and yet
      this weed grew to seed.

Mid great works of art:
   a child, hand over her eyes,
      in a pointing spin!

Still going strong
   after blocks and blocks of stops:
      my doling dog.

At the zoo

The barbed wire that pens
the old camel in, now shows
the flow of the wind.

My "How do you do?"—
is given a real answer
by the little child.

Resplendent peacock
flappingly guards his throne—
a mound of manure.

Eons of soaring,
and yet on the eagle's legs
reptile scales remain.

All is shadow now,
    except for the golden cross
        that stops the spire.

The sunset fading,
    I turn around toward home . . .
        a huge, saffron moon!

Butterflies at dusk
    drift over the garden wall
        to beds of flowers.

Drowsing into sleep . . .
    suddenly startled awake
        by a jerking leg!

Puppy gives each yawn
vocal accompaniment
to make sure it's seen.

Empty the night seems,
and yet endless flights of birds
calligraph the moon.

In a darkened room,
a spider at the window,
spinning with the moon.

Moon becoming dawn . . .
an ivory moth settles
within the lily.

The stillness of dawn:
    crashing between the branches,
        a solitary leaf.

A dry leaf, tumbling
    along the pavement . . . an edge
        to the summer air.

The ladybug graced
    summer greens, and now she rests
        at one with the leaves.

The closer I look
    into this flower, the more
        grandeur it reveals.

A real tease and sport,
   the hummingbird—and nothing
      that flies can catch him!

Now when thought ceases,
   and mind gives heed to the eye—
      a world of autumn!

Autumn . . . the path now
   wanders to oblivion
      under every tree.

A rake scrapes the walk,
   and burning leaves shape and scent
      the evening breeze . . .

This autumn grandeur!
    But for an excited bird,
        I might not have seen.

Composed of gravel,
    autumn leaves, and shifting shadows:
        the bank of this stream . . .

A berry splashes,
    then moves across the shallows
        by fits and starts.

The water skater's
    stream-bed shadow reveals
        his secret . . . pontoon shoes!

Once touching the clouds,
  now growing mosses and ferns:
    a garden of log . . .

The slippery stones
  in this stream give way to leaves
    as its depth deepens.

Consolingly white,
  the knees that the mosquito
    must bend with his thirst.

The eagle all set
  to leave—stays on to defy
    the attacking crows.

Eagle's lofty nest:
   its windy height spatters greens white
      far beyond beneath!

Never more alone
   the eagle, than now surrounded
      by screaming crows.

The Jesus bug
   skating over the stream's surface
      leaves no wake behind.

One leaf on the stream
   suddenly whirls round and round,
      and then vanishes.

At the stream's edge
a leaf drifts uncertainly,
only for awhile . . .

Bug lights on the leaf,
takes a wild ride through the rapids,
then flies away.

Autumn reflections,
within a pattern of rings
intersecting rings . . .

All of a sudden,
every bird becomes silent . . .
the sound of fall.

Autumn dawn: a flight
　　too distant to be heard . . .
　　too close for silence.

The mountain sunrise . . .
　　poised on every pine needle,
　　a jewel of dew!

Through this commotion
　　of sunbeam dust, smoke from my pipe
　　curls so gracefully . . .

That hawk on the bough,
　　now having pooped and preened,
　　looks ready for something.

Withering grasses,
   and loosening gravel slides:
      eagle's circling cry!

Standing at the summit . . .
   my dog's long hair is smoothed
      by the wind he bites.

Beyond this mountain,
   so vast as to strain the eye:
      a world of autumn.

At the summit tree,
   my exhausted dog lifts his leg;
      a dry formality.

Drifting whitely
   over a deserted beach . . .
     the sound of surf.

Smooth wet beach to run . . .
   its sand strewn with squirting holes,
     and whips of kelp!

Each kelp in the tide
   comes at last to rest, beside
     its anchor of rock.

Left by the tide
   within a shallowing pool:
     a frantic minnow.

Gulls rise as a cloud
    and fly out to sea, then turn back,
    all but a few . . .

Unrocked crabs scramble,
    only to settle down again
    with the seeping sea.

That gull in the surf,
    though deluged by breaking waves,
    always reappears!

The lofty eagle,
    lowered by hunger, becomes
    the prey of gulls.

A myriad greens
heavily laden with dew:
this oneness of frost.

The sparrow jiggles
the spider web with his bill,
then watchingly waits.

The hungry sparrow
searches the tree's remnant leaves
for one full of holes.

From a few blossoms
on the autumn plum, come fruit
for the winter birds.

These dew tiny into
   the frost—that they seemed to be
     from a distance!

Mowed grass clings briefly,
   but the fresh green smell of it
     lingers even now . . .

Through the glass clearly:
   a sparrow waging battle—
     with his reflection.

Growled from the dog's food—
   the cat leaves, taking a swipe
     at her friend the puppy.

Atop a bare bush,
spinning around on a thorn:
an empty snail shell.

Winter dreariness . . .
over the slough's unrushed sky,
a beginning rain.

Hunger drives the wren
into the dreaded hawthorne
for its blighted leaves.

Hailing suddenness . . .
the long ears of the puppy
stand at attention.

City loneliness . . .
   dancing with a gusty wind:
      yesterday's news.

Too cold for snow:
   the loneliness standing within
      each flophouse doorway.

Rubble everywhere . . .
   except for a flight of stairs
      ending in the air.

That tenement child
   performing his long shadow,
      somehow sustains the world.

Clearly heard within
the meadowlark's flight of song:
the sound of the spring.

As the first drops of
rain begin, the gentle sound
of the spring leaves . . .

How drab this rock seems,
and yet what hidden color
each raindrop reveals . . .

All the more beautiful
dewed by rain, the bloom
of your laughing smile!

From a cool splat of dew,
    with specks of yellow in it . . .
    this flowering tree!

Sun just after rain . . .
    the color of a wet rock
    fading into steam.

Each drop ringing this pool
    radiates circles of light
    on the sand beneath.

The graceful iris
    rises to bloom—a tribute
    to the soaring bird.

Plum, full of blossoms,
  yet lingering on one limb—
  a bleak winter day.

The loose end of string
  dangling from the plum blossoms
  finds bird after bird!

The blackbird puffs up
  to sing, but the best he can do
  is a loud gurgle.

Hummingbird teases,
  then escapes in a straight line
  that's full of angles!

Whatever the bird,
   the nestling's cry of hunger
     always sounds the same.

The parent robin
   always seems to know the one
     whose turn it is.

With fallen petals,
   floating on a pool of sky:
     a fledgling sparrow.

The winged darkness
   of the mourning cloak butterfly,
     has a golden dawn.

Combing out my dog . . .
  attending his ordeal,
    a whole sill of cats!

Loud frantic buzzing:
  a bumblebee emptying
    a web laced with dew.

My old sightless cat
  not only pursues flies, but
    swipes them from the air!

Now, each wisp of hair
  that I comb out of my dog
    ends up in a nest.

Robin takes the string,
  and then flies everywhere
    within the length of it!

Greedy caterpillar,
  grant it some leave to grow flowers
    for your return.

The leaf full of holes,
  fat larva crawls out on its thorn
    for his siesta.

The housecat, let in
  after a day in the garden,
    dashes to her box!

A basement of junk . . .
on a beam, free of cobwebs:
an empty cocoon.

The tomcat sniffs once
and then opens his mouth wide
and sniffs her again . . .

The grandchild runs in
to show that the hollyhock
flowers ballerinas!

The frustrated fly
drops to the window sill
and throws a buzzing fit!

A master of loneliness,
the child—so seriously
scolding her doll.

The housecat watches
the flitting sparrow, with a
chattering hunger.

Now within the house,
a new emptiness . . . I listen
with tearful eyes.

Calling grave figures
deafened by the grief of death . . .
the song, that is spring.

Cherry blossom wind . . .
   playing amongst the petals,
      a white butterfly.

Hidden by petals,
   this gravel path still leads on
      by the feel of it!

Life—a daily dream;
   and yet struggling in this web,
      how real it seems.

Now that I have freed
   the butterfly from the web,
      I feel uneasy.

Showering petals
over the path I just swept,—
grappling sparrows.

Fluttering sparrows
unite, and then try to light
on a line of web!

Following the flight
of a monarch butterfly—
the greens it reveals!

Tiny flower fly,
the one that just hovers . . .
how curious he is.

Another white bloom
  but for fanning butterflies:
    wild gardenias!

This web stays tattered,
  and yet its bugs disappear . . .
    the spider's age!

Two bugs jockeying
  about on an old leaf,
    trying to make ends meet.

Redbird won't swallow
  the bee in his beak until
    it is wholly still.

Hair on the butterfly
  is so silky it smoothes
    under stroking eyes!

The bee doesn't vie
  with the gentle butterfly,
    but finds another bloom.

The puppy's panic!
  The beetle she's been sniffing
    just climbed on her nose.

This life's full of leaves
  spat upon by a bug, that hides
    within his work.

In spite of his plea
   the sea surges up the sand,
      past the castle-builder . . .

The stilt sandpiper,
   while high and dry, has a beak
      that reaches the ground!

A sudden tickle;
   turning to brush off the cause . . .
      the edge of the sea!

A loud whisper:
   "If you don't have to go potty—
      stop dancing around!"

Sleeping puppy's nose:
    to ants—a citadel with
        a secret weapon!

Warm sand just waddles the gull;
    it's the cold beach springs
        that turn him to wing!

The gull is given
    a good shaking by the starfish
        —that he swallows whole!

Each "Time to come in!"
    turns her child's toy boat into
        a roaring dive bomber.

Old shadowy snow
   melting in a shallow pond—
   the summit beyond.

The glacial spring
   that runs rocks and cliffs, disappears
   in the wildflowers.

The eagle alights,
   and birds come from everywhere
   to scream him away!

The eagle struggles
   into flight, but once aloft—
   seldom flaps his wings.

Wild mountain cherry:
  being borne on every branch,
    the way of the wind.

The soaring shadow
  of the eagle grows immense
    within each ravine . . .

Heather, a heady scent,
  but light enough to evade
    the breath that seeks it.

The preening partridge
  stops frequently to listen
    and to look around.

All the largest trees
within this forest, have trunks
blackened with char . . .

The cantankerous crow
sleeps in a nest that's nothing
but broken branches.

Winds play on the stream,
designing the bed below
with patterns of light . . . .

One water strider,
tired of running to a stand, rests
swiftly on the stream!

The garter snake swims,
   designing the stream's smoothness
   with a wake of rings.

The snake in mid-stream
   struggles against the current, then
   decides to ride!

Calm leaves the snake's eye
   when large rocks that break the stream
   begin rushing by!

When the snake slithers
   onto the opposite shore,
   he is far downstream.

Hot sun, yet the nun
pauses to joke with a pair
of earrings and shorts.

The cashier's friendly
mynah bird, by closing time,
replies with a poop.

In a railroad yard,
bound for a world with flowers,
butterfly and I.

Rich with oil this town,
but bound by a forest that
recommends the night.

Eternity—
    in a world so brief, it isn't:
        blooming bougainvillea!

Gentle cactus blooms
    drop off to seed with a piece
        bristling with spines.

Roaring cloud of bees,
    but the trusting butterfly
        floats right through the swarm!

A sliver of moon,
    and yet within the halo
        now surrounding it . . .

A figure standing
in a garden of fragrances,
—feeling for the sun.

Swords of the iris:
all so alike, yet some bend,
talling the others.

More fall than a flight—
yet father sparrow puffs up
and sings with delight!

The fledgling alights,
and then looks for all the world
as if it isn't.

In Japan

The monastery dog
   bids the stranger welcome
   with wagging silence.

The ancient deer-scare
   now resounds—within the din
   of cars and tourists.

Before the Buddha,
   an abandoned puppy lies
   suckling the air.

On reading this poem
   of Bashō, I find myself
   swallowing hard.

Viewing the garden
more floating, than flying:
a jaunty butterfly.

Nasturtiums flower
one nectar . . . in some it's sweet,
in others, sour.

The tiny winged-bug
skating over this dew drop,
can neither stop, nor go!

The struggling ant
is suddenly unburdened
by his winged cargo!

To daddy-longlegs,
    the spines along this stem
    are covenient rungs!

This beetle running
    circles round his prey . . .
    is working up an appetite!

Ladybug struggles
    up the hairy stem—only
    to slide right back down!

The ant stepped on
    by a paw of the slinking cat,
    just scampers away.

My cast-off slipper
    has changed puppy's innocence
      into ferocity!

While being scolded
    the old cat licks his shoulder,
      pretending not to hear . . .

Dodging the kitten's
    every pounce and chase: his own
      elusive shadow.

The older cat waits
    until the trapped fly returns
      to yearn at the pane.

Milk left in my glass,
  draws the paw of the kitten
    unto emptiness.

Beaten by the heat,
  the puppy finally flops . . .
    panting silence.

The mite on this page
  is wandering his way out
    of a maze of words!

Suddenly thumping
  the floor . . . a happy moment
    in my dog's dream.

The butterfly leaves,
but the fanciful kitten springs
clutching emptiness.

The ant takes inventory . . .
then flees without a crumb
to spread the news!

Snail just raised his shell,
paused, and then dashed away
a potato bug!

I know of someone
who needs your lip service,
darning dragonfly!

Lone butterflies meet,
    flutter wildly, and then mate
        on the summer breeze.

The kitten's shadow
    is chased into exhaustion . . .
        and then just ignored.

The puppy in heat
    sits down and scoots her rear end
        along the ground . . .

A moment ago
    the kitten was full of life,
        now how limp it lies.

Flying back and forth
through the supermarket—
a frantic sparrow.

The child stops trudging,
and throws over his shoulder
—about eighty years.

One clothespin, tired of
being hung up over nothing,
just flew away!

A brassy welcome!—
Fleeing to hide, weep, and writhe:
their Hiroshima hero.

(The actual homecoming of one pilot
involved in the bombing of Hiroshima.
Now, years later, his dreams echo asylum halls.)

The soaring hunger
of the hawk wheels him, even
over the city.

In a vacant lot,
growing rows of wild flowers:
a fallen, board fence.

On the sidewalk line:
a wrecked train, being worked by
gandy dancer flies.

A dying ember . . .
in the abandoned cat, love
and the need of love.

A long line of web
  loose at both ends, riding free
    on the mountain breeze.

A spring, rippling greens
  through a dry mountain meadow . . .
    the life it gathers!

Toad commands the spring,
  but quits his stool with a splash
    before the raccoon.

Darting dragonfly
  appears aimless, while in quest
    of his unseen prey.

Deep in the mountains;
     making camp beneath a pine
     that designs the moon . . .

Night sounds of the spring,
     while beyond stretches a sea
     of myriad stars.

Sunrise: the spider
     swings on his web full of dew
     till it disappears.

The eagle's great nest
     lies safely within a pine
     the shape of the wind.

Soon bored with vastness,
I kneel to the wild flowers
and all their wonders.

How fuzzy each stem
of grass, up to where it spreads
in leave to the sun.

Like Diogenes, this bug
prefers sun to the shade
of admiration.

This fly, buzzing mad
and tumbling over the ground,
is wrestling a seed!

Exploring the way
   of this mountain spring: a snail
   with a raft of food.

Fanning butterfly,
   is the suspense you create
   part of your design?

The seed in the air
   that refuses to be caught, comes
   to a waiting hand.

That butterfly's wing
   barely grazed my cheek, and yet
   I felt his surprise!

This giant redwood
  curved through centuries, and then
    grew true to the sun.

Wind designs the pond . . .
  while beyond, a warbler sings
    in soft willow greens.

That snowy heron
  preening itself so proudly,
    has a perfect mime.

The wakeless way
  of the Jesus bug is revealed
    by lunging minnows.

Man's contribution
   to this quiet mountain pond,
      is an old beer can.

Once loudly labeled,
   now resting covered with rust,
      at one with the pond.

Cloudless moments of moon
   rippling the mountain lake,
      give cry to the loon.

Awaiting the moon;
   meanwhile the fire, this moment,
      is glowing with hues!

Somewhere in the dark,
a mountain spring rippling . . .
the cosmos beyond.

The stillness of dawn . . .
yet the leaves of lofty trees
reveal its presence.

A tiny winged-bug
feeling his way out of
a forest of hair.

Cloud shadow moves off
the alpine meadow, revealing
the play of the wind.

Bald eagle alights
on the steaming pine, then spreads
his wings to the sun.

The eagle turns to see,
but his searching eye becomes
a mirror of sun.

The beak of the hawk,
rounds all the way down to where
it can tear the air!

Deep mountain silence . . .
the distant thunder of planes,
the wail of a train.

Shot down by some kids
and now rolled on by my dog . . .
countless skies, unsung.

The fly runs over
wet leaves on his way from
the cow's steaming dung.

Fluffy dandelion
gags the sampling puppy
into coughing seeds . . .

Reaching for haiku—
on the cover, a dead fly,
and a restless seed.

The goldfinch clutches
the dry thistle, braving spines
to line his nest with down.

Hawks from everywhere
come and circle round the one
that is treading air . . .

As wonder grows on
this weed, one ceases to become,
and begins to *be*.

Now soar butterfly—
but hereafter take more care,
webs are everywhere.

Foggy mountain night . . .
   dim lights wind beyond to where
   they glow, and vanish.

In this nothingness,
   gull after gull emerges
   searching for the sea.

Now being revealed
   by every beacon moment,
   the mountain's summit.

A forest of fog—
   yet the eagle flies, squawking
   his way to the sea!

A great bank of fog:
   sea gulls emerge and then soar
    —right back into it.

Crow hops on the sand,
   but how gingerly he walks
    the barnacled rocks!

The crow in the path
   of the wafting wall of foam
    doesn't bother to move!

Harried, the eagle
   spirals from this world of crows
    to the cloud beyond.

His master returned,
  the puppy dances, sprinkling
    libations of joy.

Parakeet performs
  his high wire act, then proudly
    puffs up—and poops.

For the cat rubbing
  with love—a leg, a wall,
    even the dog will do.

To the toddling child,
  an orange is a treasure
    everyone must see!

Rumpus in the kitchen:
    scooting madly round the floor,
    a bag-headed cat!

The puppy sprawls out,
    and heaves into a great sigh—
    all that seems to be.

That flea who wiggles
    just before he jumps, is now
    somewhere on me!

Smuggled in bubbles
    up to the surface of the tub . . .
    the smell of it.

This lovely garden—
  only a short cut to what,
    haughty butterfly?

Some wandering snail
  has given this garden wall
    a real going over.

Puppy paws in fun
  beside the elusive beetle,
    then grows serious.

Puppy stops playing
  and looks around with wide-eyed
    surprise—her first fart.

Damselfly delights
 in taking cruises aboard
 the sunning goldfish.

Toad frozen with fear,
 the gnats gather in a ball
 and dance on his nose.

This black goldfish,
 swallowing the pool's surface,
 seems to be inside out.

The pair of frogs on
 this mossy stone are mating
 into their third day!

Now from dark to dark,
  clear across this autumn dawn
    is a flight of birds!

Through each sunlit leaf
  on this vine: the shadowy form
    of one behind.

A spider crouches
  at the center of this empty web,
    trusting his design.

Thorns detour the snail
  —till the rose he climbs to find
    is no longer there.

Leading ladybug
   right by the nose: the wild edge
      of this withered leaf . . .

Its long drop of dew
   falls, rolls from leaf to leaf,
      then enters the ground.

Up through rank leaves
   aging into one, this white sprout
      grew to find the sun.

The earthworm wriggles
   in confusion, but his head
      knows where it's going.

On this leaf in the pool,
    calm now casts its character
    with a graceful reed.

The tiny goldfish,
    though cruising with the others,
    stay out of their way.

Why alight, dragonfly?
    With such wings you can live
    always—on the wind.

This pool's old goldfish,
    the one with the grand tail, never
    appears anymore.

The frog jumps from pad
to pad, then hits the slit of one
and disappears.

The tireless kitten
springs to play with every gust
of the autumn wind.

A sparrow flies up
to the web, and then hovering,
looks it over . . .

What a wealth of grace
and hue, the koi searching through
this full rippling moon.

Looking like a dude
  among the autumn leaves:
    downy woodpecker.

The lowering spider
  rides out every wind
    to reach his goal below.

Sudden bird silence!
  The ground squirrel stands to hear,
    and just disappears.

As goldfinch gathers
  a beak full of thistledown,
    the seeds freed to breeze!

Level web mystery:
    solved, by seeing the spider
      that rides on the wind!

Sparrows in this storm
    fly to the tree without leaves
      and clutch its stillness.

This tiny windbell,
    now tossing so silently,
      houses a spider.

Wind just banged my gate,
    for this view through the pine
      of the rising moon!

An autumn tempest:
  just a playground for the wind,
    this turbulent world?

The leaves I kicked up
  into windy freedom
    have all gone berserk!

Pulled by wind, sparrow
  leaves the limb—for a tossing sprig
    that he can clutch.

Her kitten, too young
  for mystery, is all paws
    mid the falling leaves.

The whirlwind caught up
within that pile of leaves
must reach to the sky!

A first drop of rain
rolls around upon the leaf,
finds an edge, then clings.

My sacred windbell,
even without its sail,
is tolling tonight.

So real the world seems,
yet beyond this abiding Now,
what is not a dream?

Grieving loneliness,
   standing high above the surf . . .
      unfelt gusts of spray.

For this dandelion
   that struggled through the sand,—
      the wind from the sea.

An ebbing tide . . .
   attending its every move,
      a long line of gulls.

Crumbling with rust
   upon a deserted shore . . .
      the weight of war.

Even now, darkened
    into shape by fog, its glare
        turns away the eye.

Standing firm against
    the pull of an ebbing wave—
        in spite of the sand!

Gulls fly with the storm;
    the hawk, flapping furiously,
        struggles to remain.

The eagle stands fast
    by his aerie, scorning each blast
        from the storming sea.

Winter desolation;
  a sky of darkening gray . . .
    the splendor it holds.

Wheeling on the wind;
  an echoing shot . . . in a
    helpless fall of hurt.

A winter sadness . . .
  but my old dog comes to nuzzle
    with his kindly eyes.

Ever lingering
  in the taste of the walnut:
    deep autumn.

Come! See how fresh snow
   has silenced every edge
     of this moonlit night.

Glistening new snow;
   kids fight—then unite to build
     the fancy of one.

Chasing a bobsled
   filled with careening laughter:
     a dog barking clouds!

The old sledding hill . . .
   the thrill of its icy bend,
     its summit bonfire.

Winter reflections . . .
and yet deep within the stream,
the glow of autumn.

Gusts of powdered snow
sweep over this darkened stream
designing its flow . . .

Winter wilderness;
the wolf turns and bites into
the icy blast.

Otter play in snow . . .
ermine slinks about unseen,
its paws wet with blood.

Stalled in freezing wind . . .
  but the farmer stops to help
    with bare, insistent hands.

Shallows hold the snow . . .
  but the stream flows freely
    through autumnal depths.

Wandering through snow
  holed by drops from melting limbs:
    a path of sky.

Jonquils warm the snow . . .
  excited birds flit about,
    unburdening boughs.

Free of the city,
   my dog runs and runs until
      his tongue hangs awry.

Over spring meadow,
   playing with a fawn's abandon:
      the glacial wind.

The wild apple tree
   branching everywhere, blooms first
      among the grasses.

Deep in the mountains,
   beyond all the blights of man . . .
      the Eden we had.

Mountain meadow now
    is so tall with spring wonders,
        hawk eyes turn to rocks.

The hawk soars darkly,
    but the trailing edge of his wings
        lets the light through.

The circling hawk
    stops short, and aligns himself
        with the blinding sun.

Suddenly shadowed,
    then lifted to the sky within
        the clutch of talons!

This ancient garden
 now swept by a petal wind,—
  the scene of a dream.

Though things only seem,
 I suffer with the butterfly
  tearing in this web.

One bud on this bush
 has been chosen to awaken
  a butterfly!

Now free in the world,
 the old parakeet just perches;
  his loneliness!

Untended garden . . .
　　basking upon its sheer wall:
　　　a long garter snake.

Caterpillar climbs,
　　finds only wall, and more wall . . .
　　　then falls of itself.

The spines on this stem
　　turn the caterpillar back
　　　to its holey leaves.

Spider strides right up
　　to the glossy ladybug,
　　　stares—and then flees!

Rufous hummingbird
   standing there in the spring air
    is almost half beak!

The hummingbird veers—
   and flies right through the web,
    undewing most of it!

Signalling wildly
   for all to take care: the tail
    of the pissing cat.

Staggering around
   on this suspended petal,—
    a dizzy spider.

Level spider lines
   run across the garden, yet
     above—is but sky!

The old cat sprawls out
   in a ray of sun, then turns
     into a kitten.

Hosing the jasmine,—
   scores of startled white spiders
     bail out of its blooms!

The dangling spider
   climbs, by simply reeling in
     the line that holds him.

In a classroom . . .
   impressed upon one elbow:
   nothing-marks from grass.

In exam-silence,
   stopping trains of thought:
   a noisy stomach . . .

(*The First Principle*)

, molecules, atoms,
   now energy . . . the Buddha
   held forth a flower.

Leaving a lecture . . .
   suddenly awakened by chimes
   to a world of spring!

Flying a robin
  around the school playground:
    an abandoned kite string.

The dervishing kite—
  dives top-down right to the ground,
    then shoots up again!

The gust of wind
  that is trying on that shirt
    needs a larger size!

Sparrow on the line,
  lets loose—and finds himself
    hanging upside down.

Little chickadee's
spring assignment: all the bugs
left out on the sprigs . . .

Nestlings no longer,
father robin perches beyond
—a worm in his bill.

Lying on a leaf
full of holes: one caterpillar,
and half another.

The hopscotching child
kneels to the beetle and asks
to be forgiven.

Especially for those
who are blind to birds: the song
of the purple finch.

Going in circles
trying to make ends meet,
a frantic puppy.

Better leave the seed
until later, little bird—
a cat's in the grass.

A fall of petals—
overhead, a spider web
being worked by moon.

In a shaft of sun
  playing between the redwoods:
    a ballet of bugs . . .

The spider descends,
  dropping his line into being
    a length at a time.

A white seed wafts by,
  suddenly pauses a moment,
    then goes straight up!

Squirrel rides the bough
  into springing . . . lets go, and
    just makes the next tree.

Deer study the wind,
   then bound through the dry brush
     with scarcely a sound.

A stone throwing itself
   in the stream, then out again . . .
     the water ouzel!

At one with the silt
   the crawdad, but on each claw
     there's a shout of white.

As twilight tolls,
   petals fall into the dark stream
     revealing its flow.

Where this stream shallows
into rapids, mossy stones
harden to colors.

Half of the minnows
within this sunlit shallow
are not really there.

This bobbing blossom:
lunchtime for the minnow school,
or target practice?

Frightened crawdad runs
facing his danger head on—
while in reverse!

When contemplated,
   the egg in this nest becomes
    a treasure of browns!

The long antennas
   of the borer bug, curve round
    and end back at him!

Caterpillar moves forward
   down out of the slack
    that begins at his end.

From where ladybug
   sits on this blade of grass,
    she's above the sky!

On the cabin wall:
a pine being blown by moon,
its every move . . .

Dawn collects the dust
left on leaves by the path, into
drops of yellow dew.

A bee in a web,
whirring its one free wing
in spurts of hope.

The design that spins
the spider, allows him no rest
until it's done.

Snail, how can you move
at your embracing pace
on this blackberry vine?

The beetle's wrestle
with the old snail shell leaves him
running—in the air.

The little pill bug
folds up at the slightest touch,
and just rolls away!

Startled garter snake
defends himself with a tongue
that's rapidly red.

Hummingbird hovers
to taste blossoms, and becomes lost
in a whirl of petals!

A swift streak of gray
between greens of the garden—
the rat's fearful way.

Puppy lies wag-end up,
barking at the bumblebee
too busy to play.

The nasturtium vine
that invaded the vacant lot,
has gone on parade!

Loneliness: for the
child, an opportunity
to play Let's Pretend.

The child's dish of mud,
by her own calculation,
took a year to cook.

While scolding her doll,
the child rests her hands upon
invisible hips.

Now dusk, the spirit
of the white butterfly is that
of a dancing child.

Some spider has run
all throughout the tangled bloom
of this marigold!

For the real fragrance
of the marigold, look below
to its misty greens.

The unicorn beetle:
one of those weird contraptions
man first tried to fly!

One must kneel to see
the tiny yellow bugs that
run the creeping slug.

Lovely butterfly—
  stop drifting and settle down,
    you blur the garden.

Bumblebee covers
  each blossom of the clover
    with a buzzing care.

The leafhoppers loll
  and stagger around within
    this flower's fragrance!

Carrying the world,
  and everything beyond:
    this burdened beetle.

Long trumpet flowers
    heralded by bumblebees,
        whitely scent this tree.

The bumblebee lights,
    souses himself with pollen, then
        roars off—flying blind.

Lying on this leaf,
    yet another upturned moth . . .
        last night's full moon!

The cricket's feeler
    coated with pollen, he steps
        on it then—heads up!

Playful hummingbird
   hovers before the flycatcher,
      daring him to chase!

The enticed kitten
   positions to pounce upon
      —the dog's happy dream.

Whatever my dog
   was chasing within his dream,
      he is now sniffing!

Bitten, the thread now
   has taken a real hold on
      the kitten's rough tongue!

Mountain heat—yet here
cool scented pines hold the sun
to cathedral rays.

For the close viewer:
the still trusting splendor
of forest butterflies.

In this empty web,
left by a will to be free:
a pair of small wings.

Noisy woodpecker
is gummed-up by the old pine,
to stropping silence.

Loud resounding slap!
Finally falling to earth—
a wandering seed.

Viewing deep within
the petals of a flower . . .
its sunlit grandeur!

One ant leaves the bloom,
scrambles up the bumblebee
and sprawls in his fur . . .

It looks like the ant
that climbed aboard the bee
is going for a ride!

Single dragonflies
   are aimless enough, but that
   double-decker job!

Butterfly soars past
   her hovering mate, then flies
   backward to meet him.

Two silly stickbugs
   sitting end to end: are you mad,
   or making more?

The daddy-longlegs
   rides view-high, leaving his feeler
   to find the way.

Up close, at the place
   where spider's leg lays his line,
     there seems no design.

An eternal climb,
   and now this snail relishes
     the bread placed for birds.

Crawl caterpillar
   and fall as you will, someday
     you'll awake—and soar.

The ant's great burden,
   becomes his bridge across
     crevices in the way.

Mossy rocks linked by leaves
    from overhanging trees, give
        a song to this stream . . .

The soaring freedom
    of the swallow, like the poet's
        has its hunger.

The gnat that just rests
    upon the stream, goes unseen
        by the fish's eye.

Unlike the swallow,
    the crow takes time to perch
        when he has to poop.

This flat skipping stone
    kept for its color, appears drab
    without the stream . . .

Let the campfire die—
    we can better see the summit,
    this night of stars!

The depth of night, yet
    growing across the valley:
    the mountain's shadow . . .

Galaxies boundless
    disappear into the dawn . . .
    still the moon remains.

The last of winter
  melting in a mountain lake:
    this morning's moon.

The nameless flower
  climbing this trail with me
    is a yellow you can taste!

Frog waits as a stone
  within this mountain spring . . .
    all but his yellow eye!

Hardy ant, even
  heavily burdened you climb
    this sheer granite wall.

On the mountain wind:
the cries of an eagle
soaring far beyond . . .

The might of this pine—
splitting solid rock to thrust
its spire to the sky.

Nothing but mountains . . .
and yet with every wind,
the smell of the sea.

Swinging on a pine,—
the wild beyond echoing
my newest haiku.

At the end of this trail
now overgrown with wonders,
lives an ancient friend.

The sound of the sun
catching this towering pine
is bright falling dew.

Eagle's sparrow friend,
appears to want nothing more
than to be with him!

High beyond the trail,
entering a heavy mist . . .
the summit cloud!

Dwelling within
  an abode above the clouds,
    ancient loneliness.

A mountain vastness . . .
  feeling beyond together,
    howling summit wind.

Grown tired of being
  many men, I live now
    as that soaring bird.

Soaring on vast wind—
  winging down, up, and around,
    beyond mountains high.

Now, from the sea's edge
	to peaks clear across the sky,
		is sunset glory!

Since the eagle turned
	friend to the summit wind,
		—how easily he soars!

Summit now is all . . .
	of the world nothing remains
		but a sea of cloud.

And beyond,
	the serene realm of
the King of Emptiness
	whose infinite presence allows
		the bestowal of nothing
			save the homage
				of silence.

Poems of
THE EAGLE'S CRY

REFLECTIONS BY A SPRING POOL

From the soaring emptiness of Samadhi
I find my mind reflecting now
with the garden pool—
whose display of sky is being designed
by the dimpling stride of a Jesus bug,
and deepened by the golden grace
of the koi gliding within.
Enamoured as we are
with the dreams of becoming,
would that we might take the time
to simply be . . .
and see with wonder
as the eye of the puppy
when the butterfly flits by.
Were it enough for me to feel
with senses sharpened by concentration
this lotus moment of life.
But these poems I write
are born of a wish to share
an awareness of nature's wealth,
and more:
dimensions of being re-discovered.
Rising from loneliness
to find some ancient Chinese friends
and a cup of wine,
I pause—and in a breath
yieldingly dissolve
within the honeysuckle's
cascading perfume.

FLOW

There are footfalls on the trail,
but the cabin beyond is empty.
The old man has shared his mountain
and departed. No one remains.
Still, the summit stream flows on . . .
minnows play in its shallows,
while deep within cataract pools
the huge fish lie motionless
—though facing a current
that tunnels through boulders,
then cascades over tiers of rock
to the fertile valley far below . . .
where it widens into a stillness
which reflects the lark's flight of song
and the ocean sky beyond.

The TOUCHSTONE

Today
offers the attentive eye
such an array of autumn
as to stay awhile
even my abiding winter
of loneliness.
Thoughts, however deep,
seem a sacrilege
to the reality of this moment,
whose evanescent flow
belies its eternity.
For Now
is truly the holy time:
when and where
but in the paradisical hell
of this present
can we live even the common dream
of disparate creation?

So much for the mystic
who sings of the oneness
of all things . . .
for the time is nigh

when this truth
to life must apply.
Since dew in the web
can now mirror the light
of either sun or
man's atomic might,
there's one command
I give my Self in you:
awake to the miracle of this moment!
There's glory in the commonplace,
and more. For only now
can we grace with love
the encounters
that life offers our spirit
while it is yet unsheathed
by death.

If thought be the realm
wherein we bide our time,
with each breath do we ignore
the precious touchstone of reality:
this eternal present
of endless possibilities for awareness
and acts of sharing
—which the dying see
as alone worthy of our will
and mortality.

INDIAN SUMMER

The warm winds of yesterday
have cast a play of winter shadows
over deep autumn ground.
Yet, within my orchard garden,
Chinese roses still fountain
to where they garland the golden apples.
Flowers in shades of red remain
to design the flight of the hummingbird,
while tiny butterflies battle the wind
for each diminishing bloom.
From my home beyond I can hear
the joy of Bach, embellished now and then
by windchimes along the verandah.
A friend comes, and finding me writing
says nothing, but hands me a leaf
to examine against the light.
Serenity's fragile grace
is suddenly shattered by a motorcycle
that turns my dog Bodhidharma
into a dervish whirl of barking protest.
Suddenly in him I see myself.
For, while the contemplation of nature
smoothes the stream of mind and reveals
the wealth of this leave of moment,
waves of concern for the way of the world
ever return
to bestir my peace with sadness.

SINCE I LIVE NOW ON THE WIND

Since I live now on the wind
   wafting in from the sea,
I dread the suffocating lulls
   when both sky and land fade
   into the fuming hell of man.
The flowering hours of my garden
   once blessed with butterflies
   of every size and hue,
have emptied
   from the dancing grace of a few
   into the loneliness of one,
   to none . . .
Beauty that winged
   through eons of creation—
   decimated within a decade
by our rampaging pursuit
   of progress.

What a master of war is man—
   with death and destruction
   he is supreme;
yet how easily the blessings of peace
   are forsaken—by the ideologues

who could destroy life's dream.
But how long will fate allow us
   to tilt the world
   into an ever more cataclysmic course
   with our careening technology?
For man—the paragon—
   is so off-centering
   the wheel of life,
the sun of some tomorrow
   might well dawn
   upon the insensate prospect
   of a moonscape earth.

AS TODAY'S HOWLING STORM

As today's howling storm
   blew into the warm calm
   of yesterday
so I from youthful sweetness grew
   to this cantankerous crank
   of cynicism
whose soul aim
   is writing true
   from the depth of my being,
   for the love of you.
Some may resist such sentiment,
   but who among us can deny
   that of all the reasons to live
the highest is to give
and share with others till we die
   the treasure of our heart.

If it were fame I sought,
I would caress the flower of you
   as the summer breeze,
for none are more beloved
than the praters of love.
But in the hell of our alienation,

what does that sacred command of
"love thy neighbor as thyself"
demand
but the knowing of who
we *really* are.

And so it is
   to the root of you I'm bound,
and like the lowly worm
   that breaks the ground
   think of me that way
or not at all.
Rather, find the divine
   within your sheltered love
   of yourself,
for my own life is nothing
   if not proof
that the Holy Spirit is manifest
   in the most common of flesh.

My hedonism honed by suffering
   to Epicurean taste,
I live and write now
   as free as the spirit of Tao
   within me.

With truth as my witness
   I confess
that none rides the wild deed of pleasure
   with more willingness
   than I possess.
Moon-struck I am,
   and cunt-struck too,
for that way to the womb of life
   was made the portal of paradise
   wherein we can feel more
the ecstasy of this moment
that God gives us life to enjoy.

As the loneliness
   of our uncertain selves
   compels we seek admittance
   to each other,
know the heavenly He alone
   who passions you and me
is the One who loves,
   eternally.

RAINBOW MIST

Seeking a wilderness without words,
the way of the stream became my trail.
After hiking for hours
pack sore, and ready for rest,
I discovered this sanctuary
where falls rainbow into a pool
overflowing with reflections . . .
Eagerly, I shed my pack, boots, and all
on a bank of sand, and wade into the stream.
The shallows, so warm and soft with silt,
gradually give way to autumn leaves
and on to a rocky depth
of testicle-tightening coolness.
When numb to the waist I plunge in
and swim, soap in hand, to a ledge beyond
where I stand and lather in the sun.

After a brisk shower under the falls,
I find a warm stone and recline
into a harmony with nature
that becomes one . . . unknown.
The sun in the ledge on which I lie
caresses my back and thighs,
while its beams steam my wetness away

and swell my manhood into pleasure.
Shamelessly, I wallow
in the ecstasy of being alive.
But the burning sting of yesterday
soon becomes a begging itch,
so I slip into the coolness of the pool
and swim to where I can stand and see
all the natural wonders around me.

Beauty of a kind found within
the landscapes of Oriental art
climbs with mossy rocks and pine
up the mountain wall.
For a timeless while I stand
reflective as the stream
so by wonder am I possessed.
Then, concentrating my view within the flow
I follow the moment into
a fugal grandeur worthy of Bach:
for the sun flooding this pool reveals
crystalline streaks of blue and green
and designs the depth
with endless patterns of glow.
And dancing with this light
over the mosaic of the stream bed
are the wheeling shadows
cast by every whirl on the surface.
A school of minnows arrives, and
forms a ring of curiosity around an old can
that time has rusted to gold.

Meanwhile, on this smooth-flowing sky,
one water skater has found a fly
and is trying to hockey it
through the others. Nearby
on a large rock rushing the current,
a pair of ouzle birds are performing
their eye-catching dance, whose finale
is a plunge into the stream!
A jet streaks overhead, leaving a roar
that gradually fades into a stillness
of water sounds and forest song.
Feeling a tickle on my foot, I am found
by a baby frog who rides me back to shore.
And none too soon, for the sudden shade
of mountain dusk arrives, bringing a chill
which echoes the shriek of bats,
who wing over the stream
devouring the unseen gnats
that just a moment ago
were towering clouds in the sun.

Among all the finds of this day
the closest remain to share:
mountain flow carves its way in time
through every rock that blocks it,
while smoothing all the rest. And
would that I might have rendered this scene
with some of the reflective grace of the heron,
for I found my way of poetry here
in wildness—seen just as it is
through a rainbow mist of suchness.

A DAY OF DRAGONS

As the great bell of the monastery
tolled its last awakening knell
my abbot friend whispered:
　"Come, Mr. Daruma,
　Let us greet the sun with Fuji."

How wise those masters of reality
who divined the path should
lead disciples away from their tomb
to the mountain beyond. . . .
And though the trail in the dawn
was dark and overgrown, a blazing line
of ancient Buddhas showed the way.
Slowly we climbed beyond words and ceremony
through a wood whose calm was cadenced
by the humming of mosquitoes
and the drum of the rōshi's wind.
Finally, we arrived at a clearing
where we sat together and watched
Mt. Fuji greet the dawn.
On feeling the first moment of sun
with the summit, we bared to the waist
and performed a solemn obeisance:

one full of Zen's uncommon reverence
for this eternal Now.
Then surprisingly, at the abbot's behest,
he and I bent into a Sumo confrontation:
within the deep of his eyes
I saw my self reflected. And then
feeling him awaiting my move, I lunged
beyond contention—and enveloped him
with arms of love:

    a treasured moment of mutual embrace
    between a windbell from the West
    and a summit spirit of the East.

After I made Mr. Fuji laugh,
through the soaring view of a hawk,
we ended all the games of Zen
and simply shared the day
as dragon friends.
At dusk, we returned through rice fields
—aglow with the moon—
singing Schiller's "Ode to Joy"
along with Beethoven and a chorus
of ten thousand frogs.

By a RIVER in the AUTUMN MOUNTAINS

May these lines so embrace my spirit
that none of the contrivances of art or mind
will deter me from celebrating
this eternal moment of Creation.
For compared to the sacred suchness
of this morning in the autumn mountains,
how paltry seem the dreams of fancy
and this damnable plight of the poet
to wallow in words. And while I remain
a friend of the arts, and lover even,
I will not blaspheme to worship man
when, like the sunrise beyond,
his glory belongs to heaven.
So enough, as one devout to the Real
I cannot for long ignore the miracle play
that is Now unfolding;
a moment of communion so cosmic
nothing less than the galactic meld
of the universe and ourselves
consecrates each sip of this campfire tea.
And surely no elixir ever dreamed
could more divine the world.
For in the full savoring of this jasmine
even the most mundane teems with marvels
that beg the burnished mind for reflection.

A fully realized cup, and yet
suffused with spirit as it is, the tea alone
warms and sustains me against the chill
as I sit with my dogs atop this boulder
beside the river. Even here,
in the hardness of the granite
that surrounds my guardian friends and I,
yellow lichen has grown along the crack of time
creating an exquisite design.
Old Zen, always so patient with my pen
rests with his head upon my thigh,
while Haiku, ever alert in the wild, growls
and looks downstream with busy nostrils.
On the mountain above, sunlight
is returning to the evergreen vastness
caches of autumn splendor.
A red-tailed hawk courses through the crystal air
searching the canyon with cries that disclose
the soothing sounds of the river.
The first shafts of sun through the trees
have gradually risen into one that reveals
the hidden depth of the stream
and its clear, celadon flow.
The kingfisher watching with me, suddenly chatters
and swoops into his reflection—then
emerging with a fish in his beak
whitely wings away downstream.
Knowing this pool to be favored
by the great blue heron, I wait quietly
hoping to see again the grandeur
of its standing grace before the falls.
Meanwhile, I find myself entranced
by the endless patterns of foam

being created by the waterfall :
each drifting on the stream
to where it simply disappears
like the morning mist.

DEEP in a MOUNTAIN FOREST

Tired of the raging stream, and seeking
a way into the quiet heart of the forest,
I came upon a bridge to the wild beyond:
this giant tree fallen to the shore,
all its growth through the ages
offering an ever-widening way
into the wooded solitude I seek.
Mounting the log, I step with care,
wary lest its mosses make me slip into
a chaos of salmonberry and broken limbs.
My dogs Zen and Haiku, impatient with my pace,
suddenly race past me and on to the end.
Finally at the root, I sit
and soon find myself, like the log,
being reclaimed by nature.
Calmed by the songful silence of the forest
I come to my senses
mindlessly reflecting now—
all but its flow forsaken.
As I listen to life, I hear distant birds
echoing the song of the one above.
Haiku, now all nose and ears,
lies as a wolf among the brambles,
while the amazing Mr. Zen sits on my boot
preferring it to the damp log.
Morning sun rises through the trees
revealing the silken tie between each twig,

and warming the summer woods to scent
an essence of pine, and so much more!
Motes mingle and dance in the welcome light,
while a woodpecker rests,
deepening the stillness.
No longer lost in thought, and quieted
to where the very rhythm of nature resounds,
how blessed this present of life becomes!
Yet, what profound reluctance
now stays my pen and mind . . .
For time and separateness are gone,
and any thought—even the sharing of this—
cleaves the harmony of the one I feel
into that state of illusory "things"
we mistake for the real.

SWORN AT HEAVEN'S GATE

Feeling released from talons
after a near-fatal year,
I flow with a grateful mind
through even the raging courses
of this stream. For though bloodied
and maimed as I am,
I've sworn at heaven's gate
—with all the resolve of one reprieved—
a sacred oath to leave the way
writ with a vision worthy of my eternal eye.
(Failing this, may I be clutched again
and this time pray let me remain
with the One soaring above.)
So let the mainstream pull as it will;
I shall, like the meandering wind,
design the calm along the shore
and live now even more deeply than before
among the bamboo and flowers
of my hermitage garden. Meanwhile
know that I write not for art
or delight merely, but with the hope
my songs might reveal some measure
of the miracle this world provides.
For in the whole sweep of cosmic silence,
what celestial composition can compare
with the infinite variations
upon the theme of life within
Creation's magnificent passion
of the earth.

Having risen with the moon
  and now mindless with meditation,
    I gaze out over my wild garden and beyond
      to the glory of an ever-changing dawn.
Even as the sky now holds my eye,
  I center myself by savoring
    each sip of this tea.
Lord Krishna sprawls on my desk, purring
  with a contentment that is all affecting . . .
Through the open window before me
  a ripe plum hangs within arm's reach.
The loose vine of climbing rose
  so whipped by yesterday's wind,
now arches with a stillness
  that brings its grace of dew-brimmed buds
    to rest along the tree's one lifeless limb.
Above, among the vanishing stars
  a glad hummingbird climbs high,
    then drops in a long whistling dive, and stops
    just above the dawn.
Suddenly, he soars to the tip
  of the garden's highest branch. And there,
    with that spirited squeak which heralds
      his song of flashing iridescence,
he celebrates the sun's appearance
  over the eastern hills.

WINTER ONENESS

Soft and white upon the howling night
has come this morning of snow,
whose drifting oneness
is being given such a glory by the sun!
The barren world of yesterday,
transformed by heavenly alchemy,
now is an enchanted land
where wonders command every word.
A mantle of glistening snow
trackless but for one,
covers the orchard's withered grasses,
and every apple left for the birds
seems an ornament to the sun.
A blaze of flaming pyracantha
alone identifies the road,
where deep snow has silenced
every angle of man's offense.
And for all the burdened bushes
which appear as sculptures
unto themselves . . . it is oneness
that recommends this wintry world.
Even the great cypress
that creaked the night
now stands in snowy stillness,
a spire to the fading moon.
Bless us, for it is
one of those magical winter days,

whose like I might find
cobwebbed in the attic of my mind,
along with the old sled
on which I would play
the whole day away.

TWO DAYS

I

Among the long days of childhood
  one,
or maybe two,
    I sometimes like to remember.
Both now seem but a dream,
    and yet
how prophetic they were
    to the becoming that I am.

The first
was an orchard day,
    full of play and as free
as boyish verve could want to be.
    There was an abandoned orchard,
city-bound
    just a stone's throw
    from our school ground,
yet for us in our play
    it was worlds away.
    A time-removed
enchanted place

to my friend and I,
  where gnarled trees lowered
    their treasure-laden limbs
into summer grasses
  boy-high.
    Ripe apples and plums
hung close to hand,
  and never was fruit
    or life
    as sweet as then.

Boyish hunger finally sated,
we climbed into imagination
  and became in those trees
  Indians, sea captains,
    and Tarzans swinging free.
  So did the joys of fantasy
take our day
  that the very air and ground
  came alive with our toys . . .
until dusk
and a last call to dinner
  broke the spell.

Nearer than then
by a few years
    was a day in the wilderness,
    one that memory singles from many;
for its mountains channeled
    not only the stream of that day
    but the whole flow
      of my life.
    Till then,
nature had been but a foil for fun
    where fishing, swimming,
    and fancy held sway.
    But somehow
the events of that day
    spent with the stream
    cleared my eye of dreams
and allowed me to really see
    the actual wonders of nature
    around me.

Fish were but toys for my line
    until I saw the shallow stream
so teeming with spawning salmon
    that one ill-inclined
could step across on their backs.
    Although bloodied and torn,
they at last arrived

from the distant sea
and there,
　　circling with death,
　　were laying eggs
for more than the likes of me.
So taken I was
by their suffering mission
　　that nothing less
　　than the round of life
came through to me that day.

Nay more,
for finely keyed
　　to this new-found harmony
was my rare discovery farther downstream.
　　For there
I first found beauty,
　　poised
　　in the form of a white heron
whose exquisite thrustful stance
　　entranced me
with what has since become
　　my unending passion
　　for the Real.

INTO A MOUNTAIN EVENING

Leaving the summit to the wind,
I make my camp within a canyon
that is a confluence of streams.
From tall spraying falls
they cascade down to where
they flow together here
into this pool of turquoise
flashing with silvers, and granite-clear.
Leaving the minnows to play
with the tea leaves from my kettle,
I return to the campfire and enjoy
its embering warmth of hues.
As mosquitoes rise, I light my pipe
with a taper of sweet pine
and relax into the view beyond.
The canyon wall at dusk
is looming with the evening sun
such an array of textures and colors
it seems a tapestry of time:
the rim of trees and sky rests upon
a glowing, layered design of eons;
while in the stratas below
greens serpentine through
the ancient darks of basalt,
then range with ferrous reds
across millennial heaves of granite
and down the crags of centuries

to here . . . where voluptuous sandstones
border this flow of streams
now of a way, one.

SQUIRE CREEK

How graciously fate has tended
this stream of my childhood dreams.
For though forty years flow
between now and then, the same romance
of its woods and fields remains
as when I played here through days
that never seemed to end.

Like a spawning salmon I came,
and found my favorite pool
still mirroring its source: that peak
of wintry design known since Indian times
as the mount of the great White Horse.
No craggy challenge to conquest—
but a summit contoured by the ages,
whose majesty invites the eye
to share its repose in the sky.
Now one with the stream
the mountain rests, just as it has
in memory's serene reflection.

And still standing beside the shore,
though ramshackle and roofed with autumn,
is the cabin where we found such solace
during those dark days of the war.
While the old wood stove is gone
and only its rusty flue remains,
the incense from the orange rind
mother always placed upon its warmth
shall ever linger in my mind,
as will those simple repasts we shared.
Still, the cabin was seldom seen
for I, like the mountain,
was inseparable from the stream.

Yet how much more I see now
than when I wandered here with hook and line
and a mind cast to plunder.
Feeling a kin to the rainbows
that glide within the flow,
I wade through pools and shallows
fairly gleaming with the gold of fools:
a wealth so boundless, its specks
glint from every rock along the shore
and galaxies can be seen glistening
deep within the sky of this stream.
While contemplating this stream bed
with all its dazzle and dancing shadows
I discovered a sunken treasure:
a rare token of autumn's leave,

one so marvelously red
that the child fishing downstream
—caught by my exclaim—
came on the run to see my pleasure.
So susceptible to my glee he was
that we shared the stream together,
from crawdads and frogs to birds and trees,
till his mother finally called him home.
But the boy returned before I left
to give me the golden leaf
for which he had so deeply dived,
to wed the crimson one that I had spied.

Lest this song of the stream
seem but a hankering for bygone youth,
know in truth that I'd trade none of my selves
for the man-child I've grown to be.
And so, as lovely to me as those leaves
pressed by my heart between these lines,
is my fond hope
that I may have bequeathed to that lad
a manhood alive with wonder.

To MY OLD APPLE TREE

Whether seen along a turn of mind,
or upon this vital ground of sense,
what a worthy friend I find you are.
From some careless planting
you grew through an unshaped youth,
and sometime then it must have been
that you were scarred for life
by the tether of some spirited colt.
And while your hoary aspect well bespeaks
of a will determined to survive,
it belies a most generous heart.
For, staunch companion of my solitude,
it has been by your golden fruits
and unstinting harvest of years
that I've come to respect you
as the noblest among your peers.
Would that you could know, my fecund friend,
what a spur to my spirit you've been.
And more than once has your resolve to give
revived my flagging will.
While fate in the long run tells
what we all were meant to do,
I can see in you even now
what in myself wants so earnestly to be.
So stay awhile please,
and your deserved rest forego,
as this sheltered seedling needs
the grace of your boughs
to grow.

EDEN NOW

It is a gray day, as drifting with fog
as with melancholy about the values of man.
Scorning riches and fame, I live apart
with nature, riding the present
like a child with wonder uncontained.
Gifted by grace with awareness
wrought from sufferings,
I live as fully as I can,
my lameness and pain harsh
but blessed reminders of the real.
Agonies of mind and limb have steeled me within
against any shame at seeking pleasures.
For though we all must suffer to grow,
what treasures of life are given
to balance our woe and strife.
Why else are we here
but to mirror the glory of divine Creation?
So as children of paradise let us rejoice
in the present of life, and tend this Eden Now
with awareness and appreciation.
I, for one, find delight in the infinite sights
and sounds of nature. Of these I've sung
as simply as haiku can, for God keep me
from words that strike not the spark of life.
Let them rather be flinty and rude, and my pen
a flaming sword so as to light the mind
to wonder at the suchness of things just as they are
in the heaven of nature that surrounds us.

SHANTIH

When I arise feeling twice my age
within a cyclone of crippling pain,
I wonder if I shall ever climb
through mountain wilderness again.
Disillusionment with the world of man
haunts me more each passing year.
And there are torturous times
when this grieving combines
with my rage against the pain,
to make it all seem unbearable here.
Then, the dearness of life's dream
disappears into a longing to see
—with my eternal I beyond—
the Reality of Shantih.

DROUGHT

The pastorale of greens surrounding my home
that summered such golden harmonies with the sun
has withered to a somber mass of gray.
Cracks cleave my orchard earth, widening to where
they break the roots of thirsting trees,
and every melancholy leaf is layered with dust.
Still, miniature fruits fill the branches
—a bounty for the starving birds.
Where I once tilled vegetables with the joy
of timeless hours, only a stalk of chard remains
seeding defiantly above the weeds.
The flowers of my garden are now but a memory,
and dying grasses give ever more ground to the sun.
Fate seems bound upon a desert design.
And yet my heart is consoled
when I behold the stands of my bamboo
and their whispering greens that declare:
See here not the triumph of will, my brother,
but the grace of faith that grows through despair.

NOT WITHOUT TEARS

Dedicated to the Memory of John Farr

Not without tears
  do I recall the friend
    fate found for my becalmed years.
For his strong spirit billowed my soul
  on its journey through convention
    and beyond, to that boundless sea
      of my real identity.
Chicago tough, he rode the rails at seventeen
  and by twenty was a battle-sickened ex-marine
    seeking truths his spirit could embrace.
He was nearly thirty when we met:
  a wild eccentric, nurtured by the classics,
    with his genius flowering poetry
      from roots deepened to Buddhism.

His shack on the edge of town held
  the noblest life I'd ever found,
    for all its clutter and dogfood meals.
He then lived only to write, and came to know
  through our friend Thoreau
    that in willful poverty alone

could he find time
for the creative mind.
What a memorable mentor!
Take the day he held that Buddhist book away,
knowing I'd then read its like, and many more.
Through him I found freedom's way,
and in his awesome individuality
I saw my own hidden destiny proclaimed.

In mind and spirit did we share the years.
And cherish I will the moments of music,
sunset glory, and those discussions till dawn
that spawned our stream of creativity.
Differences there surely were,
but such scrapes—that flinty genius needs—
sparked us both to blaze
the way neither could alone.
His person was a many-faceted gem.
And as one lit with life
he was rife with contradictions.
Flawed by contention though he was,
a rare empathy shown from within
this weight-lifting mystic with a cosmic ken,
whose motorcycling, crotch-bound courage
only faint hearts could deplore.
Life was diminished by his early death,
but I know the Spirit that infused his being
lives in me,
and in all things.

A SYMPHONY OF STONES

Among those days so deeply shared
that they lend a loneliness to the rest,
I cherish most the times
when I've seen life's dream
reflected by my eternal eye
—the one of Sesshu and Hakuin.
As that autumn day in Tokyo
when a rōshi friend invited me to see
the sanctuary he found there
as a monk many years before:
a wilderness park, where chosen stones
gardened by the centuries
created a landscape of the spirit,
as mystical as those which inspired
the ancient worthies of the Sung.
Now a garden to contemplate the Tao,
we wandered sharingly through
this redoubt of the sacred wild,
whose gnarled pine
that grew stronger than a boulder
still inspires my mind.
But what I remember most from that day
was when the way designed
became isles of rock,
and we stepped out to where the pond
was reflecting all beyond.
For then, in that blessed abandon

which flows from the heart of Zen,
the rōshi conducted with masterful grace
all the myriad textures and tones of the moment
into a symphony of the stones.

ISLAND OF WILDERNESS

I

Reminiscence and Return

Soaring among the few memories
that my will welcomes to mind
is an eagle whose spiralling climb
took him to the clouds.
And as encroaching civilization dooms
this winging symbol of the wild,
I cherish that time I lived
cabined under Canadian sky
on an island of wilderness
governed by his sovereign eye.
Moated by the inland sea,
the island stretched from shore to shore
about an hour's walk across
or—if taken at wonder's pace—
a full lifetime, and more.
Although that sojourn
has long since passed, it was then
while in the first bloom of Zen
that I learned to live each day
as if it were my last.

Though lashed to melancholy
by another score of years,
I still feel the ecstatic fire
as I stand upon the island again.
With a sudden lapse into mind
I see time's providential design
in the sands being smoothed and patterned
by washes of the moon . . .
A reflection easily entertained,
but I come to my senses just in time
to meld with the dawn
that now plays over this tidepool sky.
With its glory spent, and my awareness
dashed by waves of remembrance,
I center upon the pungency of the sea
and listen to the music of life
the ebb tide stillness reveals:
from the busy sound of barnacled rocks
just abandoned by the sea,
to the cacophany of crows and gulls—
that ends when they are moved to silence
by the great blue heron's rising grace.
Were it enough for such beauty to unfold
and wing beyond—but in truth it returns,
in the swooping silence of the eagle
when he breaks his wings with a shriek
just above his prey.

And while now I write with a will subdued
by the world's suffering measure,
my continuing delight in
the unregarded miracle of life
still demands to be shared.
So, as flowers tossed upon the stream of mind
are these impressions tendered for your pleasure . . . .

A smooth wet beach, waiting to be run,
strewn with squirting holes and whips of kelp;
driftwoods, bleached and smoothed by the sea,
some etched with hunger's burrowing calligraphy;
the sand dollar's flowering star design;
an oyster shell, empty—but for the sky within.
Suddenly desiring to see the aeried eagle
—with his eye that mirrors the sun—
I make my way from the beach
through a stumble of rocks and logs
to the hill beyond, at whose base
the old trail begins. Here guardian boulders
break the ravaging sea and shore the island's rise
into a forest of giant trees.
First to the wind are the red-limbed madrones
in whose all-season majesty a few leaves
are ever adorned with autumn:
each a glow in itself, together they fire
amidst the spring and summer greens.
After a steep climb up the cliff,
breathing fades with the pounding surf
into a sylvan silence that reveals
each footfall on the path.

Now scarcely seen, the way remains
deeply blazed into giant conifers
whose charred bark has withstood
the fires of centuries.
While calm prevails within this lofty dominion,
dancing shadows give witness to the wind above,
whose vast realm now seems but an isle of azure
in an emerald sea. The great pine
whose turn it is to hold the sun
is exploding with beams—
some bejewel its boughs with amber,
while others run the silks of emptiness
down to where they strike a harmony
of undergrowth greens: from the lime of ferns
and mossy logs, to that somber palette
of autumn tints, the Oregon grape.
All along the trail, the wild rose,
so pink and simple of petal,
greets the eye . . . as does
the saffron bloom of the honeysuckle,
whose sweet embracing perfume
entwines the hummingbird's heart,
and mine. Meanwhile,
the templed stillness of the forest
so recently torn by a crow
is being rewoven by the hum of bees.

Remembering the convocation of eagles
at oyster cove, I hike through a slash

of stumps and bracken, down to the sea.
Although waylaid by the deep drum
of the rare, pileated woodpecker,
I finally arrive at the beach,
and for all the stealth of my approach,
find myself caught by the eye of eagles.
One stands watchfully over his aerie,
while others wheel high overhead
observing my every move. So distanced,
and yet warmed by their very presence,
I wade into the surging tide
over a bed glistening with the shards of ages.
Here . . . waving tresses of seaweed
hide and reveal a skirmish of crabs
amid rocks clustered with purple starfish;
the spiny rock cod that once seemed
so hideous and gray, now glides by
gleaming with scales of color
—and a universal eye!
But what really holds me is the hue
and seductive grace of the red sea anemone
as it swallows each wave of the sea.
For my spirit, too, draws upon nature
for its sustenance, now.
But how long and torturous the journey
back to the wonder of what simply
is.

II

The Eagle's Cry

Still, for all its blessings, how threatened
is the island of wilderness in this world.
So with a prayer that the eagle beyond
will echo through me his cry upon the wind,
I dare to descant this care
from his descending notes of alarm.
Man,
as your cities lay waste to the land
and industrial poisons ride the wind and tide,
as roaring machines rend
the sacred stillness of our wild,
see through your blinding pride
the blight of man upon the earth,
and the tragedy of his breeding billions
into a world meant for more than him.
Though always a danger to yourselves,
now with ultimate power and greed possessed
you threaten Creation's largesse of life.
So before your damnations of mind
make a nightmare of life's dream
—while yet there is time—
awake to the oneness of Now
and heed the eagle's cry:

THAT ART THOU.

On ENTERING the AUTUMN of MY LIFE

On entering
   the autumn of my life
my hopes and dreams for man
   are like the greens
   that graced the trees,
shrivelling
and being wasted by the wind.
While living with greater nature
   worlds away
from the urban canyons of contention,
my hopes
   for what we could be
   grow resilient as bamboo.
But when I entertain the cruel truth
of the many self-centered blind,
my dreams wither
   like fuchsias in the frost.
Would that I had never known
   sanctimonious preachers
      who bow with avarice
      before the altar of Mammon
      whom they serve;
   insecure intellectuals
      with their pedantic parades,
      whose worship of man
      ignores the command:

             no gods
        before the One.
And
heaven help us,
   yet another fakir
   from the East
is abroad in the land
selling
dazzling charms of solace
that soon darken
   into disenchantment.
Still, who can compare with
   those consummate swindlers,
   the ideologues—
   those thought-bound fanatics
who trade God's truth of brotherhood
   for power
and suffer millions to die
   for the lie of
        nation, race, or religion.

   Yet for all of that,
it's foolish to suffer the want
of a world that might never be.
So I can but try to live beyond,
   as I have,
tending the Tao within
this crucible fire
   of Now.

ON with the DANCE

While wisdom demands I see nothing
among these wafting petals
but the way of the wind,
I gladly celebrate the leave
of all those fading illusions
that flowered the spring of my life
with friends and dreams.
So as the rose opens to the sun
have I grown to embrace
the contemplative grace of solitude:
in silence serene,
without the melancholy
I sometimes feel among men,
whose world of words and ideas
can seem as alien
as some distant, ill-flung star.

Dimmed by the pall of thought,
I treasure the times
that allow the flow of Now
to flood my senses . . .
for only then can I behold
all the wonders of moment

that nature brings to mind.
Still, I feel an edge
to this summer breeze
as I see the birds beyond
vie for the fruits of every tree,
and the timber bamboo that flowers
only to die. And yet,
that such towering grace
should have come to seed
so recommends the world
that only heaven's pleasure
can tether
my enthusiastic dance with life
as it flies.

WAY BEYOND REASON

From Hellas till now
the philosophers of reason
have with abstract thought
walled themselves from the wisdom
they so earnestly sought.
To what pale avail
have these rationalists labored:
the nature of reality, of being,
still lies beyond their seeing . . .
for ultimate truth, all thought blinds.

Man's reason, his greatest pride,
can never know the realm
wherein our eternal Self abides;
the light of reason always falls short
of this One whose dream we are.
For to ponder is to wander from the Way,
and to prove—is to lose it altogether.
In metaphysical quest reason is ever blind,
for the diversity it discerns
is but a dream of its own design.
By dividing mind against itself,
it can never know the One within All

that abides in becoming.

The intellect only deceives
by categorizing this All of One
that is each moment perceived.
This NOW is a thingless flow . . .
but within the dualizing confines
of the mind which measures time,
an unreal multiplicity is contrived
which belies the true emptiness of existence.
If you doubt, just read this line
and try to find the time
or the you which began it . . .

Since it is reason's nature to theorize,
the flow of reality will always elude
its ponderous speculations:
for life is too becoming in its way
to ever be dissected
by the blunt blade of logic.
Yet rationalists remain resolute,
destitute with an uneasy belief
in a reality of their own creation.
By cogitating about life,
they conjure its constant stream

into that calendar dream
of encyclopedic fiction
most believe in, most suffer in.

The metaphysics of such men
is limited to abstractions
so carefully acquired,
for reason's categorizing mill.
The grand delusion
that learning produces wisdom,
is propagated by scholastic self-deceivers:
those intellectual malcontents
who swagger down the blind alleys
of pedantry and sophistication,
unaware that abstract wandering of the mind
only divert the soul's quest
for wisdom and rest.

All cogitation demands words,
these static symbols of past sensation.
But life is ever flux, and is never past:
a stream too swift for speculation . . . .
To think on it is to miss its flow
and the glow of its burning essence.
For only this Eternal Now *is*,

and all that seems past this Present
is a conjuring of thought:
memory is but a mirage in the mind.
And ahead of this present moment
lies only an illusory future,
the unbecome, the potential NOW.

Life's organic oneness,
when dissected by thought,
appears as a play of myriad things.
But this multitude that seems,
is only a living dream:
for we are all hollow men,
filled with the same holy Emptiness
of Him who we really are.
Separateness is but a sleep.
In truth, there are no 'things'
which live for awhile, then die.
The inner I
is that which sees itself
in all, each vital instant.
Look to NOW if you wish to know
the Tao, Nirvana, or God.

The Way lies in the falling of a leaf,
when the mirror of mind
is polished present-clear
and knows that the moment
holds all in all.
Rumination only wanders from the real
into a quandary of dualities.
Centering alone can lead the mind
to experience the Ancient One
abiding boundless
beyond this dream of time.
For in each vital moment
the cosmic play is enacted anew
by the Eternal Loneliness
of the One
who alone is true.

SUGGESTIONS FOR WRITING HAIKU IN ENGLISH

1. The present is the touchstone of the haiku experience, so always be aware of this present moment.

2. Remember that nature is the province of haiku. (Carry a notebook for recording your haiku experiences.)

3. Contemplate natural objects closely . . . unseen wonders will reveal themselves.

4. Interpenetrate with nature. Allow subjects to express their life through you. "That art Thou."

5. Reflect upon your notes of nature in solitude and quiet. Let these be the basis of your haiku poems.

6. Write about nature just as it is . . . be true to life!

7. Choose each word very carefully. Use words that clearly express what you feel.

8. Use verbs in present tense.

9. For added dimension choose words that suggest the season, location, or time of day.

10. Use only common language.

11. Write in three lines which total approximately 17 syllables. Many haiku experiences can be well expressed in the Japanese line arrangement of 5, 7, 5 syllables—but not all.

12. Avoid end rhyme in haiku. Read each verse aloud to make sure that it sounds natural.

13. Remember that *lifefulness,* not beauty, is the real quality of haiku.

14. Never use obscure allusions: real haiku are intuitive, not abstract or intellectual.

15. Don't overlook humor, but avoid mere wit.

16. Work on each poem until it suggests exactly what you want others to see and feel.

17. Remember that haiku is a finger pointing at the moon, and if the hand is bejeweled, we no longer see that to which it points.

18. Honor your senses with awareness, and your Spirit with zazen or other centering meditation. The Zen-haiku mind should be like a clear mountain pond: reflective, not with thought, but of the moon and every flight beyond . . . .